P9-DXM-975

Therapy Dogs

by Joyce Markovics

Consultant: Dianne Lahti
Therapy Animal Handler and Pet Therapy Team Evaluator
Los Angeles, California

BEARPORT

Credits

Cover and Title Page, © Effe45/Dreamstime; 4, © Eric Isselee/Shutterstock; 4–5, © Toronto Star via Getty Images; 6–7, © Marmaduke St. John/Alamy; 8, © iStock/Thinkstock; 8–9, © AP Photo/ Dolores Ochoa; 10–11, © AP Photo/Ross D. Franklin; 12–13, © AP Photo/Rich Pedroncelli; 14–15, © AP Photo/Manuel Balce Ceneta; 16–17, © Wendy Maeda/The Boston Globe via Getty Images; 18–19, © Damian Dovarganes; 20–21, © AP Photo/Aurora Sentinel, Aaron Cole; 22, © Ron Chapple Studios; 23TL, © WILDLIFE GmbH/Alamy; 23TR, © StudioSmart; 23BL, © BSIP; 23BR, © Bernard Weil/Toronto Star via Getty Images.

Publisher: Kenn Goin
Senior Editor: Joyce Tavolacci
Creative Director: Spencer Brinker
Design: Debrah Kaiser
Photo Researcher: Picture Perfect Professionals, LLC

Library of Congress Cataloging-in-Publication Data

Markovics, Joyce L., author.
  Therapy dogs / by Joyce Markovics.
    pages cm. — (Bow-WOW! dog helpers)
  Audience: Ages 5 to 8.
  Includes bibliographical references and index.
  ISBN-13: 978-1-62724-119-9 (library binding)
  ISBN-10: 1-62724-119-1 (library binding)
  1. Dogs—Therapeutic use—Juvenile literature. 2. Service dogs—Juvenile literature. I. Title.
  RM931.D63M375 2014
  636.7'0886—dc23
                                    2013032741

5545 5777   01/15

For more information, write to Bearport Publishing Company, Inc., 45 West 21st Street, Suite 3B, New York, New York 10010. Printed in the United States of America.

10 9 8 7 6 5 4 3 2 1

Contents

Meet a Therapy Dog

I'm a **therapy dog**.

I help children in hospitals feel better.

Woof!

Therapy dog

Therapy dogs cheer up people who are sick or sad.

Our owners take us to hospitals.

There we give the kids big, wet kisses.

This makes them happy.

Cats and birds can also be therapy animals.

At hospitals, sick people pet our fur.

This helps them relax and heal faster.

Therapy dogs get baths before visiting hospitals. Then they won't spread **germs** to sick people.

Therapy dogs don't just visit hospitals.

We also visit **nursing homes** and schools.

Therapy dogs wear special vests or scarves. They let people know that the dogs are working.

Therapy dogs cuddle with people at nursing homes.

We make the people feel less lonely.

A visit with a therapy dog can last as long as an hour.

Therapy dogs also visit schools.

The children practice reading to the dogs.

This helps the kids relax and read better.

Kids enjoy reading to dogs. This makes them want to read more.

How do dogs become therapy animals?

We get special training!

We learn to be calm around lots of people.

In hospitals and schools, therapy dogs must be quiet. They learn the **command** *quiet*, which means "do not bark."

Any kind of dog can become a therapy animal.

The dogs can be big or little.

Therapy dogs can be male or female.

Therapy dogs love to do their work.

They enjoy making people feel better.

It's the best job ever!

Some therapy dogs learn funny tricks to make people laugh.

Therapy Dog Facts

- Therapy dogs can work for as long as ten years.

- During training, therapy dogs are taught to have good manners and to be gentle when visiting people in hospitals.

- Some dogs that become therapy animals come from shelters. Animal shelters are places where homeless animals can stay until they find new homes.

Glossary

command (kuh-MAND) an order given by a person to do something

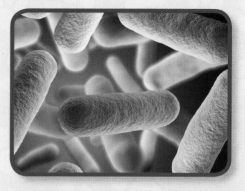

germs (JURMZ) tiny living things that can cause disease

nursing homes (NUR-sing HOHMZ) places that provide a home and care for people who are old or ill

therapy dog (THER-uh-pee DAWG) a dog that visits hospitals and other places to help make people feel better

Index

Read More

Goldman, Marcia. *Lola Goes to Work: A Nine-to-Five Therapy Dog.* Berkeley, CA: Creston Books (2013).

Green, Sara. *Therapy Dogs (Dogs to the Rescue!).* Minneapolis, MN: Bellwether Media (2014).

Learn More Online

To learn more about therapy dogs, visit
www.bearportpublishing.com/Bow-WOW!

About the Author

Joyce Markovics lives along the Hudson River in
Tarrytown, New York. She enjoys spending time
with furry, finned, and feathered creatures.